Anja Spangenberg

Little Darmstadt-ABC

Photographs by Günter Pump

Husum

Darmstadt – from the beginning

Darmstadt today is not imaginable without its history as a residence. The name probably derives from a forester called Darimund, who used to have his 'stat', or house, here. It is unlikely that the name Darmstadt has its origins in the Darmbach (local stream), another story frequently told.

At the time of the Counts of Katzenelnbogen, dating from the 13th century, Darmstadt is mainly a second or dowager residence. In 1330, the town charter was received from King Ludwig the Bavarian, implying the right to build a town wall and to hold markets. In 1479, the Katzenelnbogen's lineage ended and the territory passed on to the Landgraves of Hesse.

In 1567, Georg I settled in Darmstadt along with a small entourage of 19 servants and 17 horses. This marked the beginning of Darmstadt as a residence. Building activities proliferated and many of the buildings exemplifying the town-scape originate from this period. These include the residence, the Old Town Hall, the City Church, the Herrngarten and the Große →Woog. From 1678 onwards a time of hunting activities followed under the Landgraves Ernst Ludwig and Ludwig VIII. Several hunting lodges around Darmstadt as well as the one found in →Bessungen and the →Orangery give testimony to this era. Not only architecture but also culture and esprit grew. The Landgravine Caroline was corresponding with Frederick the Great and Voltaire at this time, as were many others. Hence, Darmstadt turned into a meeting point for the literary avant-garde, the circle of the Empfindsame – age of sentiment – which surrounded Merck, Goethe, Herder and Wieland. Landgravine Caroline's son became the first Grand Duke Ludewig I by Hesse and by Rhine in 1806. During his reign, he granted a constitution to Hesse. He commissioned Georg →Moller to expand his residence. Moller drafted buildings including the Grand-Ducal →Theatre, today's House of History; →St. Ludwig; the Freemason's Lodge and a whole district with prestigious residential homes. The English Princess, Alice, brought new impulses in 1863 when she promoted a nurses' training school as well as better education and job facilities for women. The last sovereign, her son, Ernst Ludwig, appointed artists to create the unique Jugendstil ensemble on the →*Mathildenhöhe.* Darmstadt became the capital of the State of Hesse and the state parliament was situated in the city. Darmstadt remained the capital until 1945. In 1937, the last Grand Duke died when he and his family were killed in a plane crash. On the 11th September 1944, 80% of the city centre was destroyed in the 'Brandnacht' and 12,000 people died. Wiesbaden, which was scarcely affected by war damage, became the new capital of Hesse after the war. Thus the post-war period demanded two different types of reconstruction. The buildings had to be rebuilt but also a new identity had to be developed by the citizens during the 'Darmstädter Gespräche'. Former military areas were converted to house 'smokeless industries' such as publishing houses. Literature shaped Darmstadt in many ways as the German Academy for Language and Poetry moved to the city. Since then the renowned literary prize, the Georg-Büchner-Preis, is presented

every year in Darmstadt. Many writers like Matthias →*Claudius*, Georg and Luise →*Büchner*, Ilse Langner, Elisabeth Langgässer, Ernst Kreuder to Gabriele Wohmann and Karl Krolow have lived and worked in Darmstadt up to today.

Since 1997, Darmstadt is called 'City of Science', a title due to the GSI Helmholtz Centre for Heavy Ion Research; the Fraunhofer Institute; the →*Technische Universität Darmstadt;* the ESOC and many other institutions working in the city. With about 140,000 inhabitants, Darmstadt is still a tranquil city with many parks and gardens. One can easily picture the vineyards which used to be on every hill of the city.

Achteckiges Haus

The Achteckige Haus is of a rather unusual shape, having eight corners; it also has an unusual history. It is situated in Mauerstraße. The name of the street reflects the house's history as the town wall used to run along its course. Ludwig V built it at the beginning of the 17th century in a beautiful garden area. Shortly afterwards, he made a present of the house to his chancellor, Wolff von Todenwarth. Von Todenwarth asked the architect, Jakob Müller, to give the building its now characteristic octagonal shape. In 1760 it again changed hands and its new owner, Ludwig IX, gave it to his mistress, Helene Martini. After her death his successor, Ludwig X, used it for storing wood. A few years later a small hospital opened and the building was then run by nine young doctors who mainly treated eye diseases. The house achieved historical importance when Grand Duchess Alice bought it and opened a nurses' training school. It was the first non-academic school for training young women and became a great success, despite only having a capacity of ten beds. The hospital expanded and transferred to new premises and a public bath-house moved into The Achteckige Haus. Subsequently, Baptist worshippers used it for their assemblies. Since 1992 the Darmstadt concert choir and a jazz club have used the building.

The Achteckige Haus was probably built in 1630 as a garden shed situated in a garden next to the town wall.

Arheilgen

Arheilgen, an area which is situated to the north of the town of Darmstadt, has been visited by many famous travellers on the journey to Frankfurt or Heidelberg throughout several centuries. Goethe stayed several times while visiting his friend, Johann Heinrich →*Merck*, who owned an estate in Arheilgen until his death. When you look at the old customs office, Schreiberpforte, which was en route for commercial travellers aiming to trade in Darmstadt and at the inn Goldener Löwe, you still get an impression of Arheilgen in former times.

For centuries, Arheilgen was apt to be divided one way or another. In

Above the entrance to the former inn 'Zum weißen Ross' a plaque has been placed for Johann Wolfgang von Goethe and his friend Johann Heinrich Merck who bought the house next door in 1788.

The Schreiberpforte dating from 1648 succeeded the former Customs Office. Around 1775 the inn 'Zum Goldenen Löwen' was built. The decorative portal is reminiscent of the Jugendstil.

the 13th century the counts of Katzenelnbogen ruled the older part while the masters of Münzenberg ruled the more recent part of the area. At the beginning of the 20th century, the German-French border ran through Arheilgen and complicated everyday life considerably. Farming was the main occupation of the inhabitants until the pharmaceutical production of Merck moved into the area. Since then, Arheilgen has changed from a rural village to a working-class estate. In 1937 Arheilgen lost its independence and became part of Darmstadt.

Battenberg

The Battenberg family, now better known by the name of Mountbatten, originate from Darmstadt. Grand Duke Ludwig II married the princess Wilhelmine von Baden. Their marriage was not very happy and Grand Duchess Wilhelmine moved to the nearby residence Heiligenberg. Georg →Moller enlarged it according to her plans. In the next few years Prince Alexander and his sister Princess Marie were born there. It is said that their father was the cavalry captain Senar-clens-Grancy. Tsar Alexander of Russia was on tour of Europe looking for a wife and, by chance, met Princess Marie. They fell in love with each other and had a messenger sent to Tsarina Catherine II to seek her consent to marry, which she granted. Prince Alexander of Hess fell in love with Julie von Hauke and married below himself against the will of his family. Later on Ludwig III bestowed the title of Princess of Battenberg on her and thus made it possible for them to resume their position at court. Their son, Ludwig von Battenberg, entered the British army and became First Sealord. As it became impossible to have a German officer in this position he had to take his leave. King George V consequently changed his name to Louis Mountbatten. Lord Louis Mountbatten was assassinated by the IRA. The widely visible Golden Cross on the Heiligenberg was erected by Marie and Alexander to commemorate Grand Duchess Wilhelmine.

The Old Mausoleum on the Rosenhöhe where Prince Alexander is buried

Peter Behrens

Peter Behrens planned his first house for the exhibition Ein Dokument deutscher Kunst, which opened in 1901 on the →*Mathildenhöhe*. He was already well known as a painter of the Munich Disaffiliation (Münchner Sezession). Grand Duke Ernst →*Ludwig* had become aware of Behrens and asked him to come to Darmstadt. Peter

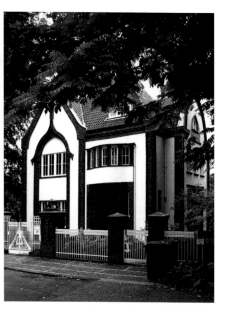

Behrens lived in Darmstadt for five years together with his wife Lilly and his two children. Lilly received several awards for her creations of coloured fancy paper and her designs of reform dresses. Behrens' house is the only one of the artists' houses on the Mathildenhöhe which was not designed by Josef Maria →*Olbrich*. It has an almost sacral air to it with its lines striving upwards and its impressive entrance door. The unity of design of the house and its furniture were met with great approval, particularly that of the public.

In 1903 Peter Behrens became director of the Düsseldorf School for Arts and Crafts. He then moved on to Berlin, where he became a member of the Arts Board of AEG. He designed almost everything for them ranging from houses and kitchen appliances to advertising brochures. Thus, he was creating the company image and worked as one of the first industrial designers. Amongst the architects he employed in his Berlin office were Walter Gropius, Mies van der Rohe and Le Corbusier – some of the most important architects of the 20th century.

The 'Haus Behrens' on the Mathildenhöhe

Bessungen

Walking through Bessungen today you enter a lively part of Darmstadt with twisted streets. You may come across the Henkershaus, where the executioner and his family used to live, or pass the →*Orangery*, a terraced garden. In the 19th century all of this lay well beyond the town wall of Darmstadt as Bessungen was a mere hamlet with vineyards and gravel pits. Small craftsmen lived here who supplied the court with their goods earning a meagre living.

A look into the history of Bessungen reveals that it is situated at the crossroads of two important Roman roads. There has been an independent parish church since 1002, known today as Petrus-

In the 18th Century the executioner Schönbein's family lived here.

The hunting lodge was built between 1709 and 1726. The premises include stables, a kennel and a dog parlour.

kirche. The village developed slowly until Landgrave Ernst Ludwig discovered hunting as a new pastime. He built a hunting lodge to house his guests during the hunting season and added stables for the numerous horses, a kennel and a cellar to keep the slain deer as cold as possible. All this lasted for a hundred years until Landgrave Ludwig IX ran out of money. In the meantime civil servants had begun to build their houses in the cheap area of Bessungen. Chancellor Moser bought the Prinz-Emil-Schlösschen, added several plots of land to it and created a landscaped garden. It consisted of ornaments like a small temple and a pond as well as an extensive kitchen garden. The uninhabited hunting lodge was converted to accommodate soldiers. A parade ground was cre-

The small castle was built in 1776 for the state reformer and writer Friedrich Carl von Moser (1723-1798).

ated and Bessungen developed into a garrison village. The incorporation into Darmstadt brought new schools, water supply and the tram to Bessungen at the cost of its independence.

Nowadays, the highlight of the year in Bessungen is the funfair, which is situated around the Brunnebütt, when the Lappings, as the people in Bessungen are called, celebrate exuberantly. The name Lapping (from French: lapin = rabbit) originates from the time when Georg I bought rabbits and set them free to breed, which they did very successfully.

Botanical Gardens

Many prospective visitors to the Botanical Gardens, seeking the entrance, try their luck at the so called 'Beautiful Gate', a wrought-iron gate which was created as the main entrance at the end of the 19th century. Nowadays, the entrance is situated a few metres down the road. In 1841, the first Botanical Gardens of Darmstadt were opened in the castle moat. Until then, the moat had been fed by the Darmbach, which carried all the sewage of the neighbouring old part of town. The court gardener, Johann August Schnittspahn, created scientifically designed gardens. He was the first of a dynasty of gardeners from the Schnittspahn family (to shape the garden). As the moat was rather narrow, the gardens were moved to the nearby →*Herrngarten*. Two further moves had to be endured before it was settled in an area east of the city in 1874. Shortly afterwards, the Botanical Gardens became part of the → *Technische Universität*. Its aim is to please as well as to serve scientific research. Some features are worthy of a visit, such as the listed entrance building with its wooden spi-

ral staircase, drafted by Karl Hoffmann, a Darmstadt professor of architecture, in 1902. The garden covers an area of 4.5 hectares, including several hot and cold greenhouses. It owns an extensive collection of groves, some of which are over one hundred years old. A big variety of cacti, succulents, pot plants and the Clusia can be discovered and admired during a walk around the grounds. A sand dune has been created to preserve the variety of plants which could be found on the sand dunes around Darmstadt. This is a special rarity worth looking at.

Breweries

Wine was among the favourite drinks of the Darmstadt citizens for a long time. Vineyards flourished in privileged locations such as the →*Mathildenhöhe*. Beer is first referred to in the chronicles in the middle of the 16th century, when the Darmstädter Hofbrauerei in the palace is mentioned. More than one hundred years pass before commercial brewers enter history. In 1715 the brewers' guild was formed. At this stage, some 28 breweries existed plus numerous small brewing businesses. Their co-existence led to a lot of trouble. Some breweries look back on a long tradition like the inn 'Grohe'. Grohe started in 1711 and is a traditional brewery and pub. Another house, the 'Goldene Krone', was taken over in 1756 by cellar man Johann Wiener. Today, it is the oldest remaining inn in the city. The brewery of Johann Wiener, the 'Wiener Kronenbräu', was built on top of the tunnels and cellars that were dug into the hill of Mathildenhöhe. The adjoining beer garden is still one of the most popular as it offers generous trees in hot summers. Nevertheless, the brewery

Old brewery tower in Dieburger Straße

ceased production fifty years ago. Another well known emblem is the 'Rummel-Locomotive', which is still to be seen on the labels of the bottles of the 'Darmstädter Privatbrauerei'. Jacob Rummel founded his firm in 1847 close to the old stations. A rather recent launch is the 'Ratskeller-Brewery' at the market place. In its cellars and on the benches outside there is room for many guests.

Büchner

Darmstadt and the name Büchner are linked in various ways. Georg Büchner, who is the best known of the family, visited the →*Pädagog* here and wrote 'Danton's Death', under the watchful eyes of the constables. He escaped them by climbing over the back wall of his parents' garden with the help of a ladder he had placed there in anticipation. A plaque commemorates this event. During his lifetime, two of his siblings were much more famous than him. His brother, Ludwig, wrote a philosophical book called 'Force and Matter', which went through 20 editions, where he propagated a purely materialistic conception of the world. In consequence, he lost his post as a Private Lecturer at the University of Tübingen and returned to Darmstadt, where he worked as a physician. His sister, Luise, became celebrated through her publication 'Women and their Vocation'. The first edition was printed anonymously and later editions bore her name; female authorship was no recommendation when she began to write. The sub-ject was the necessity for better education for girls, in order to enable them to earn their living. Luise co-operated with Grand Duchess Alice on several projects which are still in existence. The origins of the Alice Hospital and the Alice-Eleonoren-Schule – Eleonore was added under the last Grand Duchesse Eleanore – commemorate their committed efforts for better learning and working conditions for women. Ludwig and Luise are buried on the Alte →*Friedhof*.

Central Station for Electric Light

In 1888, only a few years after the opening of Thomas Edison's first power station in New York, Darmstadt built the Central Station for Electric Light. Originally, only the production of direct current was technically possible. As direct current could only be transported over short distances, the station had to be built where the electricity was going to be used: close to the palace and the residential theatre. Only a few households nearby were also supplied with electricity. Franz Frenay had to enlarge the building in 1896; a second building was added in 1906. Today we can still see the machine hall with its cambered roof and yellow clinker. Next to it is the former boiler house. The roof is constructed of glass, so that, in the event of an explosion, it night blow off, thus reducing damage to the rest of the building. By 1920, the production of electricity in the centre of town had to be terminated, as the capacity to extend the power station was limited. Until

1979, the halls were in use as control units for public transport. The buildings were renovated and restructured in 1997. Space for a food hall

The Central Station offers space for readings, concerts, theatre productions and exhibitions.

and a variety of restaurants and cafés was created in one building. In the other building the Central Station Company offers lectures, concerts, theatre performances and exhibitions on several floors.

Matthias Claudius

If you are in Darmstadt during a moonlit night, you should take a stroll around the back of the →*Vivarium*, along the Schnampelweg. Under an old oak you will find a wooden panel with an inscription of the poem by Matthias Claudius, 'The Evening Song', beginning with the famous line: 'The moon has been arising'. Matthias Claudius is supposed to have written it during the time he lived in Darmstadt; probably close to the bench you are taking a rest on enjoying the scenery. Matthias Claudius stayed for only a year working for the Grand Duke's administration. Unfortunately, he was much less suited to this work than to writing. During his time in Darmstadt, he published a newspaper called the Hessen-Darmstädtische privilegierte Landzeitung, aimed at the rural population. In order to gain their attention he invented the figure of the invalid sergeant, Görgel. This enabled him to introduce topics in their language which otherwise would have been censored. One of his masterpieces concerns a deer which describes its experience during a coursing and is looking for sympathy with its fate. Being unhappy in Darmstadt, Claudius left after a year and returned to his home in Wandsbek.

Close to a bench overlooking the Darmbach, Matthias Claudius is said to have written his famous 'Evening Song'.

Darmstadtia

Cities usually have a patron saint to protect them from all kinds of rigours. Darmstadt's patron saint is called Darmstadtia. Her statue was created by the stonemason Johann Baptist Scholl the Younger. He used yellow sandstone from the region. Originally, the statue stood in the middle of the Ludwigsplatz but was removed in favour of a statue of Bismarck. She makes a martial impression with a sword in her right hand, the buckler showing the city arms; she has a crown on her head. Today, she can be seen in the cellar of the Alte →*Pädagog* where she watches the patrons of the restaurant. A replica was put up in the →*Wolfskehlsche Garten*, so anyone looking for her protection can visit her at any time.

The patron saint Darmstadtia was originally cast by Johann Baptist Scholl the Younger. A copy by Karl J. Buchert is situated in the Wolfskehlsche Garten.

darmstadtium

By 1994 Darmstadt became known internationally. In 1994, the GSI Helmholtz Centre for Heavy Ion Research discovered a new ion which resulted from the fusion of copper and nickel under high velocity. It was named Darmstadtium (element 110). Darmstadt became the only German city to have an element named after her. A decade later the newly built congress centre in the heart of Darmstadt was consequently named 'darmstadtium'. The impressive dark building, reminiscent of a stranded ship, was planned by the Viennese architect Talik Chalabi. Local people

The impressive building was designed by the Viennese architect Talik Chalabi.

call it the 'bendy box'. The central congress hall and 18 further congress and seminar rooms offer flexible space for events ranging from concerts and other cultural events to scientific congresses or trade fairs. Remains of the city wall dating from the 16th century were discovered during its construction. They include a defence tower and a tunnel used for eavesdropping on enemies. A small exhibition has been mounted on its history. A tour through the building will reveal the complicated construction of steel and glass, showing the uni-queness of each window. The calla sharped construction placed in the centre of the darmstadtium is worth seing as it serves as a means to supply the centre with fresh air as well as with rainwater, thus improving its ecological balance.

Datterich

An original Darmstadt character is the Datterich. He was created by the writer Ernst Elias Niebergall. Niebergall was born in 1815 in Darmstadt. He studied theology at the county university in Gießen. On his return to Darmstadt he earned his living as a private teacher. However, he had another talent and began writing plays. Two years before

his death the Biedermeier burlesque 'Datterich' appeared.

The leading character of the Datterich was a boozy law assistant called Friedrich Hauser. He suffered all day from a 'vasteckte Dorscht' – meaning he always felt a wee bit thirsty, desperately needing a drink. Hauser's employer, the supreme revenue authority of the Grand Duke, discovered his habit and sacked him. In the Datterich his state is then described as being 'discreteer, at the moment without office'. It comes as no surprise that the poor man had to finance his visits to eating houses and pubs by incurring debts and by sponging off his fellow men. The smart sarcasm of the play as well as its dry sense of humour has made it one of the most popular dialect burlesques in Germany. The policemen in the play are the only ones who speak proper German as the censors feared policemen speaking dialect might make them less respected.

ERNST ELIAS NIEBERGALL

The Datterich Fountain with its moveable bronze figures and quotes from the play

Both entries to the municipal library have a monument dedicated to Niebergall. The fountain in the Große Bachgasse was created by Well Habich in 1930. The turning sculpture on the side entrance shows the main characters of the Datterich along with their best known lines. It was designed by Bonifatius Stirnberg.

Eberstadt

Reading the name Eberstadt one might guess a connection to the wallows of wild boars (Eber); this is confirmed by the impressive bronze boar next to the Town Hall. Nevertheless, Eberstadt's name originates from quite a different event. 'Stat' refers to a dwelling, circa 782, that was inhabited by a man named Eberhard. The hamlet was first mentioned in the Lorscher Codex as 'Eberstadt im Oberrheingau'. At this time, Walther and his wife, Williswind, endowed their property

to the abbey of Lorsch. In the 13th century Adelheid von Weiterstadt brought Eberstadt as dowry into her marriage with Konrad Reiz von Breuberg. He built the castle →*Frankenstein* and called his dynasty after it. People in Eberstadt lived as farmers, tanners or worked in one of the water mills. A walk along the Modau still gives testimony to the long milling tradition. Several of the inns offered lodgings and refreshment for travellers on their way to Heidelberg. The old church – Dreifaltigkeitskirche – which is situated on a sand drift and the tim-

In the oldest district the former brewery and the cooperage Diefenbach are situated.

bered houses in the Oberstraße, still give a good impression of what Eberstadt used to be like. A new mansion settlement was started around 1900, north of Eberstadt. Walking through this area of comely mansions evokes the picture of its original inhabitants: wealthy upper middle class people. Above the settlement area the sisters Isadora and Elizabeth Duncan ran a dancing school. Nowadays, a secondary school uses the buildings. Eberstadt became a district of Darmstadt in 1937, but still is a very independent district with an original character.

Electric and other trains

From 1846 onwards a railway line over 95 kilometres in length connected Darmstadt with Heidelberg and Frankfurt. The Main-Neckar-Rail used steam locomotives that ran twice a day to Frankfurt and three times to Heidelberg. Ten years later,

The main station that was completed in 1912 is regarded as unique.

the first trains of the Hessian Ludwigsbahn started their service on the line Darmstadt–Aschaffenburg. The next services led into the Odenwald, from where the much-needed workers travelled into Darmstadt; also goods left Darmstadt by rail to all destinations. It was a proper rag-bag of companies, all operating from one square. There were constant delays of trains or coaches, with travellers, more often than not, missing their trains as they couldn't reach the station in time. Around the turn of the century, it was decided to move the stations further out of town. The central station was built according to the plans of the architect Friedrich Pützer, and all the tracks were transferred. The address 'Am Alten Bahnhof' preserved some of the atmosphere of the old station square. When the central station was electrified in the fifties, five bridges had to be lifted for the installation of the mains.

The train museum in Kranichstein is worth a visit. On the site of a shutdown station the history of electric and other types of trains becomes 'hands-on', with almost 150 carriages being restored and ready for use.

In the railway museum more than 45 locomotives and over 150 wagons are on display.

There are several journeys every year on the tracks belonging to the association running the museum. Another focus of the collection is in the field of street-cars and their predecessors, the steam street-cars, which originally connected the districts of Darmstadt to the city. Some of them, such as the 'Feurige Elias', run regularly through the city on their 'steam-days'.

Empfindsamkeit
Age of Sentiment

The →*Herrngarten* is not only the green lung of Darmstadt, it also served as the background for a circle of poets and muses who promenaded through its environs during the age of Empfindsamkeit at the end of the 18th century. The soul of the Darmstadt group were the court officials Andreas Hesse and Johann Heinrich →*Merck*. On numerous visits Johann Wolfgang Goethe and Johann Herder, along with Martin Wieland and Sophie von La Roche, became part of the group. Their muses were 'Psyche' – Caroline Flachsland, who married Herder; 'Urania' – Henriette von Roussillon and 'Lila' – Louise von Ziegler. They spent their time with the poets, went into raptures over the beauty of nature and indulged in friendship and moonlit walks. There are various literary pieces giving accounts of this highly emotional period, including some by Goethe as well as several collections of letters and poems by various members of this group. Reading them makes the vibrant atmosphere of the Empfindsamkeit tangible, a contrast to the existing stiff

court etiquette. Goethe called the group 'Gemeinschaft der Heiligen' – Community of Saints. They often spent their time walking around the Herr-

gottsberg. They carved their names into one of the rocks which was a sacred place to them. Today it is called Goethefelsen.

The Goethe Monument in the Herrngarten, showing a youth symbolizing the genius of poetry, was created by Ludwig Habich.

The Felsings – a dynasty

Most Germans will know the four 'Fs': frisch, fromm, fröhlich, frei (fresh, prous, cheerful, free) – the motto of the 19th century gymnastic movement – but most will not know that they originate from Darmstadt. Johann Heinrich Felsing, nicknamed the 'Hessian father of gymnastics', created them. Johann Heinrich Felsing is a descendant of a family with three generations of famous copperplate printers and copperplate engravers. His father, Johann Conrad Felsing, was apprenticed by the Darmstadt copperplate engraver Göpfert. When Göpfert committed suicide, he took over the print shop. Thus Felsing copperplate printshop took up trade in 1797. They printed portraits, maps and book illustrations. Both his sons, Johann Heinrich and Carl Jakob Otto, were trained

Johann Heinrich Felsing was one of the founders of the Darmstädter Kunstverein – Art Society.

by him and attended drawing classes by the well known architect Georg Moller. Johann Heinrich went to Paris for his further education and led a detailed correspondence on printing colours with Justus von Liebig. He was interested in galvano technique and in paper production. In the end he added the line of original graphics to the firm's products, which enhanced its reputation. His brother Carl Jakob Otto went to Italy for his studies and was honoured for his etchings, which

The grave of Johann Heinrich Felsing is on the Alte Friedhof – Old Cemetery.

were in the manner of classical paintings. On his return to Darmstadt, he took over the printshop. He was one of the founders of the Darmstädter Kunstverein. The Florence Academy appointed him professor. His son, also named Carl Jakob Otto, went for further studies to London after his apprenticeship with his father. Printing original graphics for artists like Max Klinger, Käthe Kollwitz, Heinrich Zille and Max Liebermann, became the main field of work for the firm. The grave of Johann Heinrich Felsing can be visited on the Alte →*Friedhof* in Darmstadt.

F Fraa Liebig

Standing in the shadiest corner of the Luisenplatz, looking at the sculpture of a woman sitting on a pedestal and reading the name Justus von Liebig on the plinth, one is sure to conclude her to have been his wife. If, then, a Darmstadt citizen passes and mentions 'Fraa Liebig' – Mrs. Liebig – matters seem to be clear. You have probably guessed it already. The monument has been erected in memory of the famous chemist, Justus von Liebig, who was born in Darmstadt in 1803. But, it has nothing to do with his wife. The art nouveau artist, Heinrich Jobst, designed the monument as an allegory for the idealised figure of science. She is holding a small bronze figure in her stretched out hand, seeming to bare a number of breasts or testicles. It is meant to celebrate fertility and acknowledge one of the most famous discoveries of Liebig: meat extract.

Liebig was not very successful to begin with. He left the local Latin school, →*Pädagog*, without a diploma and did not finish his apprenticeship as an apothecary in Heppenheim. Due to the good connections of his father, he

Liebig is omnipresent in Darmstadt.

was admitted to study chemistry in Bonn. He continued his studies in Erlangen and Paris and was appointed professor of chemistry at the county university in Gießen at the age of 21. In 1852 he was appointed to a post in Munich. He was called to Darmstadt as a medical-technical expert in the murder case of Countess Emilie von Görlitz. He explained that it was out of the question that a body could inflame itself, concluding that the countess must have been killed. Liebig did not only discover chloroform but was instrumental in the development of fertilizers. Traversing Darmstadt, you will encounter his name on badges, street signs and public buildings.

Frankenstein

Every year in October a rather eerie group of characters appears inside the old murals of Frankenstein Castle. You may be reminded of the monster, created by Baron Frankenstein in the story by Mary Shelley. But these people are not connected with her story but are there to give people the creeps. The castle's story began a long time before Mary Shelley's day, when Konrad Reiz von Breuberg had the castle built, in 1252, to protect his estates in the region and to house his family. Soon, two lines of the family lived within the castle's walls, which led to numerous quarrels. They even divided the village of →*Eberstadt*, at the foot of the Frankenstein, into two parts in order to separate their income. Continuous trouble with the Count of Hesse-Darmstadt over tolls, hunting rights and mills made the von Breubergs finally sell the castle to him in 1662. The castle's history became chequered. It experienced various fates from being used as a prison, a forester's lodge and a shelter for invalids and then to rediscovery of the castle, which was by then in ruins, by the Romantics. The state of

The castle ruin Frankenstein lies south of Darmstadt.

Hesse had the ruin secured in 1970 and a restaurant with a lovely view over the Rhine plane was erected. The 'Frankensteiner Eselslehen' still reminds us of

the time of sovereignship of the Frankensteins. It was the custom in Darmstadt to send for a donkey on Shrove Tuesday. Wives who had beaten their husbands were then sat on it facing backwards and led through the city. The Frankensteins received 12 malters of corn and 4 Hellers in return until the powers that be in Darmstadt thought this too costly and had a wooden donkey substituted.

Friedhöfe – Cemeteries

Cemeteries are often the most beautiful parks in cities. Hidden behind red brick walls of the Alter Friedhof – old cemetery, you can discover a fine selection of old trees and tombstones carved by famous sculptors like Well and Ludwig Habich; Georg →*Moller*; and Johann Baptist Scholl the Elder and the Younger. The tombstones reveal the wealth of the deceased as much as the flavour of their time;

Grave stele of Moller

many stones have Art Nouveau elements. From 1828, the dead found their last resting place in this cemetery, an avea previously used to mine grit. The first cemetery of Darmstadt was situated behind the Stadtkirche in the centre of town. One tombstone of this first cemetery can still be seen as it has been built

Grave of Charlotte Heidenreich von Siebold

into the wall of the church. During the plague epidemic in the 17th century, half the population died; hence the cemetery became too small. It was moved to the nearby Kapellplatz, where you can still see a few old gravestones. As population kept growing rapidly, this cemetery was soon overcrowded and a new area had to be found: the Alter Friedhof. The villages of Eberstadt, Arheilgen, Bessungen and Wixhausen faced the same problems and all built cemeteries during the 19th century.

Some 60 grave-sites of honour are to be found in the Alter Friedhof. Amongst them are the graves of renowned Darmstadt citizens such as Georg Moller, Josef Maria →Olbrich, Kasimir Edschmid, Luise →Büchner, Elisabeth Langgässer, Charlotte Heidenreich von Siebold and Erika Köth. Some more important grave-sites are

Friedrich von Flotow died on 24th January 1883.

in the 'Waldfriedhof' – cemetery in the forest, which is situated west of Darmstadt. You can walk to the graves of Albin Müller, Dorothea Hollatz, Erasmus Kittler, Carlo Mierendorff and Paula Ludwig. The Jüdischer Friedhof – Jewish Cemetery with Arnold Mendelssohn's grave is another one worth a visit.

Tombstone of the writer Luise Büchner

LOUISE BÜCHNER
GEB. 1821 . GEST. 1877

Gas and water

Walking through our cities nowadays, it is difficult to perceive the manner in which households are supplied with daily water and electricity. Everything which is now invisible was originally conveyed over ground. Gas supply started in Darmstadt in 1848, about fifty years after gas was first used in a lighthouse in Le Havre.

The gas which was obtained to facilitate cooking in the Darmstadt area was delivered in containers. Every day inns and tradespeople received their gas in this way. In 1855 a network of pipes was constructed, mainly to supply the gaslights in the inner city. Every evening the night watchman leaned a stepladder against the lampposts, climbed up and lit the lamps. In the mornings he had to go on his tour again and extinguish them. During the summer the lampshades were taken down as they were popular targets for a good throw with a pebble. In 1962, more than half the streetlamps in central Darmstadt were still fuelled with gas. In 1966, the production of gas ceased in Darmstadt and from then on gas

The reservoir can be visited on a guided tour.

came through long-distance pipelines.

The water supply started off in wooden, later clay, pipes which ran from the sources around Darmstadt to the city's wells. The system was never sufficient and there were numerous water shortages. Sewage ran openly on the street's surface until it ended up in the castle moat. If it hadn't rained for a while the filth

stank in the streets. If the rain came pouring down, a ghastly mud developed, which people had to wade through. As a first improvement stone slabs were put down at the end of the 18th century and drains were built. There remained the problem of the poor water quality and its unreliable supply. As population increased rapidly a solution had to be found. Finally, in 1880 a water reservoir was built on top of the →*Mathildenhöhe*.

Water from Griesheim was pumped up by steam engines and could then flow down to supply households. At the same time a sewage network was constructed. The first water closets were installed inside houses. By the time of World War I, the new water supply system had led to an increase in the consumption of water from 39 to 150 litres per person. The old water reservoir on the Mathildenhöhe can be visited on guided tours.

Gefängnis – Gaol

The most prominent victim of the pitiable conditions in the old prison of Darmstadt, the Arresthaus, was the priest Friedrich Ludwig Weidig. He was remanded in custody for the second time in 1835/36 as he was accused of treason against the Grand Duchy of Hesse. As co-publisher of a publication called the Hessische Landbote he had demanded a united and democratic Germany. The first time he was arrested he had been lucky that the coroner – a well known choleric – could not convict him of being the author. The second period of custody was lethal for him. After having been maltreated and suffering from the unbearable conditions of the imprisonment, Friedrich Ludwig Weidig finally committed suicide. On the morning of the 23rd of February 1837 he was found lying in his own blood on the floor of his cell, still alive. But even many hours later no doctor came to see him and he finally died. His tombstone on the Alte →Friedhof was boarded up by officials claiming its visitors caused trouble. It had, in fact, become a symbol for the opposition movement for the injustice inflicted upon Weidig. In the revolutionary years 1848/49 the boarding was taken down and a vow was taken to protect the tombstone 'for ever'. A plaque on the remains of the walls of the old Arresthaus reminds of the incident.

Remains of the old prison's walls

Haus der Geschichte
House of History

Today the Haus der Geschichte is a calm place but it has gone through glamorous and eventful episodes. It was built as the new Grand-ducal →*Theatre* in 1819 by the architect Georg →*Moller*. With an auditorium that seated 2000 spectators, it was one of the biggest theatres of its time. The whole city was crowded with carriages and no inn or hotel had a free room left on the days performances took place. People came from Frankfurt, Mainz and even as far as Heidelberg to see a performance. As the Grand Duke was particularly fond of

The former Court Theatre was built in 1819 following the plans of Georg Moller.

opera, many were in the theatre's repertoire. He often could be seen with his back to the audience while he conducted the orchestra. In 1871, the theatre burnt down to its outer walls after an illuminator had forgotten to extinguish a candle. Gottfried Semper drew plans for the reconstruction but, in the end, Georg Moller's plans were used for a second time, though slightly altered to include some necessary improvements. As the theatre was reopened, it became a public magnet again. It burnt down for a second time during the Brandnacht in 1944. This time it stayed a ruin until, in 1986, the city decided to reconstruct it. The theatre had, by then, found new premises. Thus, it was decided to house a variety of archives dealing with local history and to let some rooms to the historic society of Hesse. To make the Haus der Geschichte more attractive to visitors, the vestibule was designed as an exhibition space. On the first floor the impressive Karolinensaal is used for festive concerts and functions.

The foyer is worth a visit. It has been rebuilt in the style of 1879.

Haus für Industriekultur
House for
Industrial Culture

The façade of the Haus für Industriekultur tells of its industrial origins but doesn't give away the trade. With four storeys and a clinkered front, it reflects the wealth of its owner, Ludwig Alter. He supplied the court with exquisite furniture which he exhibited in the Artists' Colony on the →Mathildenhöhe. Starting in 1906, he first sold furniture to wealthy customers. During World War I he changed his line of production to interior fittings for aeroplanes and railway carriages. In order to find more customers, he later started mass production. Nevertheless, the firm had to be closed down in 1929. Opel used the premises for many years to store spare parts. Since 1996, the premises

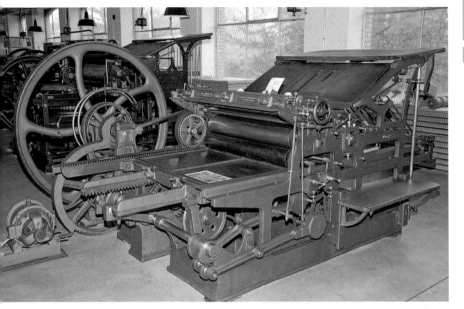

The museum is an active place. You can experience manual typesetting, printing machines and artistic flat printing.

have been open to the public. A branch of the →*Hessische Landesmuseum* has an exhibition on printing, type-setting and the casting of fonts on display. All processes concerning printing, ranging from a cast-iron hand-press to a bookbinder's workshop, have been bequeathed by the largest European typefounder D.

Stempel, Ltd. Apart from exhibition cases, there are workshops or demonstrations on various techniques, including book-binding, hand-setting and gravure printing. The development of printing from hand-press to modern printing technologies can be pursued and experienced.

Herrngarten

Passing between the →*Haus der Geschichte* and the →*Hessische Landesmuseum*, a cast-iron gate leads into a wide park with huge old trees, wide lawns, fountains and fine sculptures. You are entering the Herrngarten, the former palace garden. In the 16th century it was still next to the palace. Fruit and vegetables were grown in the Landgrave's garden. He even planted hops and kept bees. Part of it was designed as a pleasure garden, where members of the court enjoyed walking and conversing in the lovely surroundings. In the 17th century Landgravine Elisabeth

Dorothea had a wall built around the garden, some parts of which still exist. She changed the design into a formal garden. Only a century later Landgravine Caroline changed the design to a landscaped garden following the English garden tradition. She felt so much at home in the garden that she had her gravesite built in it. She is buried there. The gravesite was later decorated with an urn presented by Friedrich II of Prussia. He admired her intellect which, at that time, was perceived as being equal to a man's. The engraving says that although Caroline was physically a woman, mentally she equalled a man. At the beginning of the 18th century the garden was opened to the public. To begin with, constables kept a close eye on their behaviour, as they tended to leave the paths or drop their litter onto the immaculate lawn. Today, the park is used all year round for walking, physical exercises and by students preparing for their lessons. People of all ages enjoy this generous haven of tranquility in the centre of Darmstadt.

The Herrngarten is the oldest park of the city.

Hessisches Landesmuseum – Hessian State Museum

Between the →*Herrngarten* and the castle a rather special museum is situated. It was built in 1906 by Alfred Messel. Grand Duke Ernst Ludwig was very dedicated to this project as he wanted a building to accommodate his extensive collection. The result is a universal museum where sections covering many topics can be found. The displayed artefacts stem from the accumulated items of the royal family. Landgravine Caroline set up a cabinet for minerals. Subsequent generations added new objects according to their interest. Some bought at random, others systematically. In 1805, Baron Hüpsch endowed his extensive collection and others followed his example. In 1820, Grand Duke Ludwig I donated his precious items to the state as he wanted the public to be enlightened and entertained by them. In 1874, the archeological finds from the Grube Messel – Messel Pit Fossil Site – were incorporated as well with objects such as the Propaleotherium parvulum and the anteater which had been found in the oil shale. The collection today offers dioramas on the habitat of animals, a geological-mineralogi-

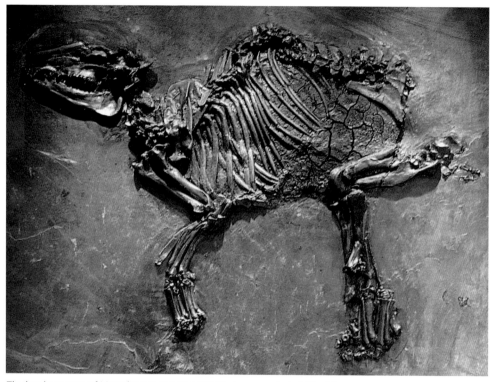

The local museum of Messel presents a view on life over a period of 47 million years.

cal section, as well as a physical cabinet. The works of art range from the Block Beuys to Simon Spierer's 'Forest of Sculptures'. Two more branches belong to the museum: the →*Haus für Industriekultur* which focuses on the history of printing and the folklore collection which is displayed in the Museum Centre Lorsch.

Jagdschloss Kranichstein – The hunting lodge Kranichstein

The nobleman, Henne Kranich von Dirnstein, who was enfiefed with a hermit's lodge in 1399, lent his name to

A bronze stag in front of the hunting lodge

the farmstead. A golden crane, symbol for the name Kranich, is today looking from the roof. Landgrave Georg I purchased the farmstead in 1572 and commissioned Jakob Kesselhut to convert it into a hunting lodge with a model farm. The farm was to ensure food supply for the people in Darmstadt. Georg I fenced in a game-park and reforested the area with pine trees, for the forest had been ravaged, for a time, no landgrave had been resident in Darmstadt. Local farmers had to fulfil their labour service by digging out the Backhausteich in which to breed fish. Georg I introduced clover as a feed crop so animals could be fed all year round; he also set free rabbits and planted the first Borsdorfer apple trees. Under the reign of the Landgraves Ernst Ludwig and Ludwig VIII, the hunting lodge had a glorious episode. Landgrave Ernst Ludwig was a dedicated hunter and introduced par force hunting. This demanded quite a number of stables for horses and kennels for the well trained dogs. The animals were required in large numbers, as the hunting covered long distances. Extra dwellings for the guests had to be built as well. The wide reach of the

The Backhausteich in front of the impressive silhouette of the hunting lodge (see next page)

par force hunting required star-shaped forest aisles to offer a good view for the spectators. A circle of smaller hunting lodges was built in the region, including ones in Bickenbach, Ernsthofen and Mönchbruch. In 1768 Landgrave Ludwig IX ended this passion for hunting and sold all he could to balance finances. Kranichstein stayed the summer residence of the court. Today, a museum on the history of hunting in Darmstadt is within the old building and there is a considerable collection of weapons. One wing of the building accommodates a hotel and a restaurant. The former hunting arsenal is now housing the Bioversum, a museum on the protection of species.

Justiz – Justice

Standing on Mathildenplatz, enjoying its tranquility, with the plastered paths leading up to the impressive lion fountain, you will find yourself surrounded by law courts. The first law court – the Justizpalast – was built on the north side of Mathildenplatz in 1874 opposite the Neue Kanzleigebäude, where all ministries were to be found. It is worthwhile taking a look at the classical front and a graffito by Eberhard Schlotter, which is situated in the hallway that was added in the middle of 19th century. A few years after the completion of the first building, a second one was built on the right hand side, housing the district court. The inner courtyard is impressive, with its milk-glass ceiling and a copious hallway surrounded by galleries. The buildings are linked by the

The entrance hall of the district court is a special gem with its inner court covered with a milk-glass ceiling. The foyer is characterised by one of the most beautiful staircases in historical (neo-Baroque) style in Hesse. All three floors have arcades with round arches surrounding them.

so called Seufzerbrücke – bridge of sighs – to avoid having to leave the building. Continuous lack of space led to the construction of the Neue Justizzentrum – New Centre of Justice – in the year 2000. The importance of the building is conveyed by the arcades of fundamental rights. Twenty-one articles of the German Constitution are replicated and illustrated by photographs. On top of the roof, Justitia stands accompanied by a labourer and a bourgeois, watching the independence of law with covered eyes.

The Wilhelminian buildings which were built in 1906 and 1872 are connected by a bridge. On top of the roof Justitia stands accompanied by a labourer and a bourgeois.

Kollegiengebäude
Council Hall

The impressive building on the north side of the Luisenplatz, showing an expansive baroque front, is the Kollegiengebäude. After the old chancery had burnt down in 1715, the government and the administration had to cope for many years with cramped facilities. Landgrave Ludwig IX finally commissioned a new building for all ministries. He asked the Hanau Oberbaudirektor Franz Ludwig von Cancrin to draw the plans. In 1779, the Kollegiengebäude was completed; Darmstadt's oldest administrative building. At a total cost of 83,000 guilders it turned out comparatively cheap. At the same time, the Hessian County Theatre was built at the cost of 600,000 guilders. Today, the →*Haus der Geschichte* – uses its building. From the start, there was insufficient space in the new building to house all the ministries. Hence, additions were built by Georg →*Moller* in 1825 and 1845. For 230 years public authorities have been in its representative walls ranging from the Grand-Ducal court of Starkenburg and the Home Office to the Ministry of Justice and, today, the Regional Council.

Lichtwiese
Meadow of Light

The bright name conceals a rather dark past. Until the end of the 15th century, the whole area of today's Lichtwiese was covered with a deep forest. When the forest was cleared, light could enter and cattle were set out to grass on the pasture. The name, however, probably derives from the tax that had to be paid in lights or candles. Part of the area was used by the merchant, Karl Netz, in the middle of the 19th century, to grow mulberry trees for his silkworm breeding. In one corner, the new cemetery was opened. In another part, a society called 'Darmstädter Privilegierter Schützenverein', settled and, as they used their area to practice shooting, they ran into trouble with the visitors to the adjacent graveyard. Finally, the shooters moved to Griesheim and the dead could rest in peace again. For some years, a society for naturopathy ran an air-light

bath here. The 20th century brought more change to the Lichtwiese. The university stadium was built in 1919 and, from 1926, regular flights to Munich left from the airport, Darmstadt-Lichtwiese. In 1934, flights were relocated to Griesheim for safety reasons. Today, much of the area is covered with buildings of the →*Technische Universität Darmstadt*, linked by an extensive sculpture park.

Wide areas of the Lichtwiese are covered with buildings of the university; a sculpture park spreads among them.

Literaturhaus
House of Literature

Literature needs space to live in, for reading and listening. The Literaturhaus of Darmstadt found this space in 1996 in the former John F. Kennedy House. On four floors, all kinds of archives and libraries can be used; rooms for lectures and readings are available. The range of libraries is from the Elisabeth-Langgässer-Society to the Lichtenbergsociety and the centre of the German PEN – poets, essayists, novelists. Writers meet in the 'Centre for young literature' or the 'Textworkshop'. Listeners attend readings organized by the Literaturinitiative. Small libraries like the Louise-Büchner-Bibliothek and the Alexander-Haas-Bibliothek found facilities in the house as well. Furthermore, cultural associations from India, Italy and Bulgaria have their offices next door to the Foto-Club, the Art Archive and the Chopin Society. A bi-annual brochure informs on the readings. Over the years authors like Anna Enquist and Wilhelm Genazino have read from their books to an interested audience. Events on Matthias →Claudius or Carola Stern took place. It would be easy to spend a rainy season in the Literaturhaus without once getting bored.

Not only the Literaturhaus focuses on books in Darmstadt. Some of the most distinguished literary prizes are awarded in Darmstadt, such as the renowned Georg-Büchner-Preis, the Johann-Heinrich-Merck-Preis, the Leonce-und-Lena-Preis, the Ricarda-Huch-Preis as well as the Kranichsteiner Literaturpreis. They are awarded in numerous venues all over Darmstadt, such as the German Academy for Language and Poetry.

Löwen – Lions

'Well roared, lion!' one is often tempted to call out to a lion with wide-open jaws while taking a walk around the city. Already the Jews called Darmstadt 'Löwchen Mokkum' – city of the lions – because of its numerous beasts. An impressive number of lions can be found on doors, windows, manhole

The city arms (on the wall of the old town hall) date from the 15th century on seals. It goes back to the Counts of Katzenelnbogen. Two lions wait in front of the Hessian State Museum. The coat of arms is depicted on manhole covers.

covers, fountains and sockets. The reason for the great quantity of lions is not that Darmstadt used to be an

of Katzenelnbogen. Most of the lions are of a different type; they look striped and only have three claws on their paws. In this instance they are Hessian lions and are present on all official buildings of the former residence and capital of Hesse. Once you start looking for lions, you will find it difficult to stop and you will definitely enjoy the hunt, as the variety is charming.

agreeable habitat for these beasts, but the fact that lions symbolise power. The oldest lion can be seen on the city arms. It appears in the company of a lily, carries the Grand-Ducal crown and is a scary red lion, with four claws on its paws; this representation has its origins in the coat of arms of the Counts

Ludewig and Luise

Not even death can separate Grand Duke Ludewig I of Hesse-Darmstadt from his Grand Duchess, Louise, after fifty years of marriage, thanks to the citizens of Darmstadt. He is looking down from a 39 metres high column onto the Luisenplatz – Luisensquare. This is one of the reasons why, in Darmstadt, the monument is often called 'Long Ludwig' and the monument's real name 'Ludwigsmonument' is scarcely known. Once a month its doors open and there are 172 steps to climb, with the reward of a wonderful view of the city. The money for building the monument came from the citizens as a reminder of the constitution Ludewig issued.

Georg →*Moller* drew the plans for it and under Ludewig I he built a whole new quarter. Ludewig began his reign as Landgrave Ludwig X and received the title of Grand Duke from Napoleon for his participation in the Confederation of the Rhine. That Luise would become his bride was not altogether certain as it was intended that he should marry Sophie of Württemberg. Tsar Paul II intervened and claimed Sophie, so her cousin Luise was then considered. Luise not only gave birth to six surviving children, but also en royed an extensive corre spondence with the French Queen, Marie Antoinette.

The 39 metres high Ludwigsmonument is situated in the middle of Luisenplatz (next page). The square was named after his wife.

Marketplace

Two squares in particular form the character of Darmstadt: the Luisenplatz and the marketplace, the latter, having always been in the same place, is the oldest square of the city. The site of the marketplace fountain, which used to be right in the middle of the square, gives a clue to the original extent of the area, showing that it has doubled in size. It was built to supply the citizens with water, as only a few

houses had their own wells. From the beginning of the 13th century, markets were held every week and a trade fair twice a year. Bakeries and butchers – with their slaughterhouses – surrounded the market. The marketplace was used for announcements of the authorities; it also served as a place for jurisdiction and punishment. The gallows and other instruments of torture stood there. Under the reign of Georg I, 37 people were burnt to death, having been accused of witchcraft.

Originally the market fountain stood in the middle of the marketplace.

To the south of the square is the old town hall; to the north the →*Residence*. In the 19th century a Jugendstil

building was erected on the west side to house the first department store. It was founded by the Rothschilds; later Henschel & Ropertz took over their business. Today, the market-place invites you to linger a bit longer, visit one of the cafés, enter the cellar of the local brewery or buy some fresh fruit and vegetables at one of the stalls.

Martinsviertel

In Darmstadt, the Martinsviertel (Martinsdistrict) is often called 'Watzeviertel' – district of the boar. This does not refer to the inhabitants' lack of cleanliness, but it evokes the local boar, the 'Watz', who had his service sty in the district. The oldest houses were built under Georg I in the former pear gar-

den, during the first extension of Darmstadt. He wanted them to be respectable looking, so he demanded the front to be built of stone. To be able to afford stone in the 16th cen-

The beautiful Renaissance facades in the Martinsdistrict are worth a visit.

tury, the owner had to be very rich, as transport costs were expensive. Behind the façade, common local materials like straw, timber and clay were used. A group of the neat Renaissance facades is still preserved in the Alexanderstrasse. In the middle of the 19th century, a huge number of labourers were moving to Darmstadt, urgently looking for lodgings, which were created in the Martinsviertel. Walking through this district, you will, therefore, discover many houses of the petty bourgeois. On the fringes of the district tenements with historic fronts are predominant. The atmosphere of the area is largely influenced by students from the nearby university, with a lot of pubs and small shops selling uncommon goods.

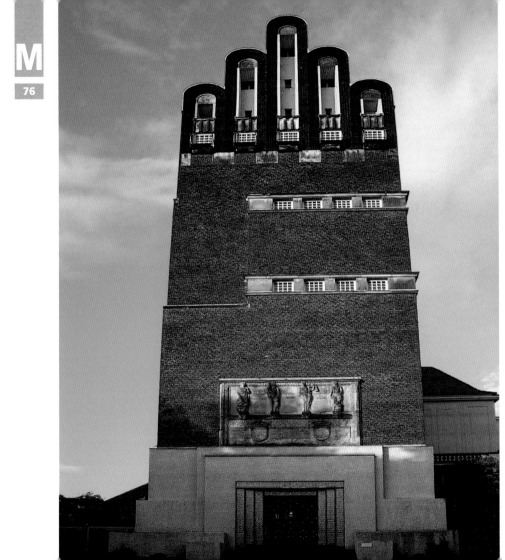

Mathildenhöhe

From the centre of the city you can already see the top of the Hochzeitsturm – Wedding Tower – with its crown of five fingers protruding. It is the landmark of Darmstadt and was planned by Joseph Maria →Olbrich, on the occasion of the second marriage of Grand Duke Ernst Ludwig, to Eleonore of Solms-Hohensolms-Lich. His first marriage was to Princess Victoria Melita of Edinburgh, nicknamed 'Ducky', the grand-daughter of Queen Victoria. The city's wedding present to the couple was the tower. Today, it is used as a branch of the registry office in accordance with its name. The ceiling of the entrance hall is decorated with a mosaic called 'The Kiss' and is by Friedrich Kleukens. If you climb the stairs, you reach a visitors' platform that has a panoramic view. Until the beginning of the 19th century, the Mathildenhöhe was a vineyard. Later, the Grand Ducal family converted it to a landscaped garden. On the occasion of the marriage of Princess Mathilde of Bavaria to Ludwig III, she received the park as a wedding present. To honour her it was named Mathildenhöhe. She had the Platanenhain – plane tree grove – planted and this still survives. During the 19th century, wealthy citizens began to build their villas on the west slope. An elevated tank for the

In 1908 the 48 metres high Wedding Tower was completed. On its red clinker is a sundial on the south side quoting a poem by Rudolf Binding.

Playing petanque under the plane trees

water supply of the city was erected, which from the socket of the Ausstellungsgebäude – Exhibition Hall. In 1897, the →*Russian Chapel* was built, following the plans of the Petersburg architect, Leontij Nikolavic Benois. The glorious period of the Mathildenhöhe began in 1899, when Grand Duke Ernst Ludwig appointed the first seven artists under the leadership of Joseph Maria Olbrich, each of them receiving the title of professor. Cheap plots of land were made available to them and they were instructed to build artists' houses for themselves. Ernst Ludwig became acquainted with the Arts and Crafts movement during his visits to his royal relatives in England. By founding the Artists' Colony, he had in mind a connection between

Art and Crafts and the wealth of local workshops. In 1901, the first exhibition, 'Ein Dokument Deutscher Kunst', was opened on the Mathildenhöhe. The public took great interest in the artists' houses, which had been created as a synthesis of art. Each of the artists' designs was integral to their particular characters and interests; the houses were to fit like a second skin. From fences and eaves to lamps and furniture, everything was designed with floral or decorative elements. Reactions from the public were often restrained and Jugendstil was scarcely copied in contemporary buildings.

Three more exhibitions took place on the Mathildenhöhe in the following years. In 1904, the Dreihäusergruppe –

The Platanenhain was designed for the exhibition in 1914 by Bernhard Hoetger.

group of three houses – was created as an example for bourgeois living. In 1908, the 'Hessische Landesausstellung für freie und Angewandte Kunst' – Hessian State Exhibition for Free and Applied Arts – took place; works of art and handicrafts from the whole state were on display. Reminders of this exhibition today are the Hochzeitsturm and the exhibition hall. After the death of Joseph Maria Olbrich in 1908, Albin Müller took over the artistic leadership of the Artists' Colony. The themes of the fourth and last exhibition were the Platanenhain – plane tree grove – and the artistic decoration of the

The swan temple was built as a tea-house.

Lilienbecken – basin of lilies – that were built to integrate the Russian Chapel with the Mathildenhöhe. Bernhard Hoetger created a group of sculptures under the topic of the 'Circle of Life' for the Platanenhain. Its central sculpture is a replica of the

tombstone of Paul Modersohn-Becker's grave. The group was destroged diering the 1944 Brandnacht – night of fire – and only partly restored post war. Since the middle of the 1970s, the ensemble is gradually being reconstructed. During a walk across the Mathildenhöhe, surprising and charming details lurk in every corner. The spirit of the Mathildenhöhe is still alive as it continues to convey some of the euphoric mood at the beginning the 20th century.

Merck

The name of the family 'Merck' has been linked to Darmstadt for centuries and in numerous ways. In the beginning, the family of the pharmacist, Merck, moved to Darmstadt and bought the Angel Pharmacy near the →*marketplace*, in 1668. The first member of the family to become famous was Johann Heinrich Merck in the 18th century. A writer of various kinds of literature including reviews, he also worked as a naturalist. In the field of zoology, the 'Rhinoceros Mercki', illustrates the variety of studies

he undertook. He was very fond of the Arts as well. He was the first to print Goethe's "Götz von Berlichingen" in an author's edition. It was due to his efforts that Goethe, who was then still little-known, joined the 'Darmstadt Circle of the →*Empfindsame*', which wrote poetry together, celebrated

The gravestone for Franciscus Merkius is situated on the premises (left). On the tombstone he is praised as 'de arte pharmaceutica merentissimus'. The premises (above) are decorated with an entrance tower by Friedrich Pützer.

nature and gave way to their passions. Working as a court official, Merck had to cope with the contradiction between court etiquette and his position as an enlightened man, an inner conflict which

culminated in suicide by pistol. His grandson, Heinrich Emmauel Merck, was more successful with his ventures. In 1827, he introduced his 'Cabinet of Pharmaceutical and Chemical Innovations', the foundation for today's global enterprise, Merck. The production of alkaloids and fine chemicals advanced the rapid growth of the firm. At the beginning of the 19th century, it had outgrown its original space in the city and relocated to the north of Darmstadt, to →*Arheilgen*. Today, a tower designed by Friedrich Pützer, and a blue shimmering pyramid, grace the entrance. With over 300 years of company history, Merck is the oldest pharmaceutical-chemical company in the world.

Moller City

The most influential person for the structures of the city of Darmstadt was the architect Georg Moller. He pursued his studies at Christian Ludwig Wittig's and Friedrich Weinbrenner's, then travelled to Rome. At the age of 26, Grand Duke →Ludewig I called him to Darmstadt in the position of the Grand-Ducal Court Architect. Hesse-Darmstadt had just become a Grand Duchy. This meant more power and more territory but

One of the buildings erected according to Moller's plans is the classical extension of the Kollegiengebäude (1825). The house has been reconstructed after World War II.

also more bureaucrats and more citizens. Thus, Moller's task was to build a new district to the west of the city. The roads and squares he planned were so generously laid out that they could cope adequately with urban development for the next 150 years. Buildings had a classical design and symmetrical fronts. On the ground floor, windows were often designed with a round arch. The facades were dignified with a cornice running along the front and a balcony facing the street. The overall height was the "Mollermaß", a three-storey construction. In his position as Court Architect, Moller signed all construction plans of the city and the region and took care that his standards were met. The following were built in Darmstadt according to his plans: →St. Ludwig; the Masonic Lodge; the Hessian County Theatre, today's →Haus der Geschichte – House of History; the Palais Prince Carl; the New→Kollegiengebäude; the old Mausoleum on the →Rosenhöhe and the Ludwigsmonument in the heart of the city. This lead to an omnipresence of Moller's buildings in the inner city, although the Brandnacht of the

The Freemason's Lodge was opened in 1818.

11th September 1944 destroyed most of his residential houses. He was the first curator of monuments in Hesse and focussed on the preservation of historical monuments; among other things he prevented the demolition of the Carolingian Lorsch Gate House, also known as Königshalle, which is now listed as a UNESCO World Heritage site.

Neufert's residence for singles

At the foot of the →*Mathildenhöhe* you can see a high, clinkered building. Clinker is not a typical building material of the region; nevertheless it was used to cover the walls of one of the five realised Meisterbauten – masterbuildings – in Darmstadt. At the end of World War II, the city asked eleven renowned architects to develop drafts for the reconstruction of schools, nursery schools and hospitals. The only residential house that was built from these drafts was designed by Ernst Neufert. Neufert was a trained bricklayer and carpenter. He had studied with Walter Gropius and finally taught at the Bauhaus. In 1936 his Bauentwurfslehre – 'Architect's Data' – had been published; still an important reference concerning building standards. The university gave him a professorship in architecture in 1945. In Neufert's residence for singles – Neuferts Ledigenwohnheim – in Darmstadt – often called the 'bull's fortress' – the occupants were mainly bachelors living in small apartments. The flats had a superior standard of living. The complex included a laundry, a restaurant and some hotel rooms. It was recently modernised to meet current requirements. One apartment was left with the original amenities. Neufert drafted one more building in Darmstadt: the hydraulic engineering hall of the →*Technische Universität* Darmstadt.

Olbrich

Joseph Maria Olbrich has influenced, to a great extent, the appearance of the →*Mathildenhöhe*. Following his apprenticeship in bricklaying, he then went on to study architecture at the Viennese Academy for Arts and worked as an assistant in the office of the architect, Otto Wagner. Thus, he completed a sound education for an architect of his period. He made a noise in the world, being one of the founders of the Vienna Secession. He became famous for his draft of the building of the Vienna Secession, one of the central works of the Jugendstil. Grand Duke Ernst Ludwig appointed him head of the Artists' Colony in Darmstadt, in 1899. For the first exhibition, in 1901, Olbrich drafted the following buildings: the Ernst-Ludwig-Haus, housing today the Artists' Colony Museum; the Große Glückerthaus, today home of the Deutsche Akademie für Sprache und Dichtung – German Academy for Language and Literature – and the Kleine Glückerthaus, owned privately. Both Glückerthauses were used by the Darmstadt furniture manufacturer, Julius Glü-

The German Poland Institute is situated in the Olbrich House.

ckert, to display furniture. Furthermore, Olbrich designed the House Christiansen, which was bombed during the war; Haus Habich which is owned privately; Haus Deiters and his own house, which are both used today by the German Poland Institute. He influenced the 'Darmstädter Jugendstil', which is mainly based on the conviction that a house should be built according to the needs of its inhabitants; it should surround them

O
87

like a second skin. The response of the public was divided, so Olbrich mainly worked for the Grand Duke in subsequent years. Further buildings he planned for the Mathildenhöhe after 1901 are the Dreihäusergruppe, the Ausstellungsgebäude – Exhibition Hall – and the Hochzeitsturm – Wed-

ding Tower – his last piece of work in Darmstadt. Olbrich and his work were trail-blazing for his time. His oeuvre ranges from drafts for interior decora-

The Große Glückerthaus (above) is the seat of the German Academy for Language and Poetry. The central portal of the Ernst-Ludwig-Haus was opened at the first exhibition in 1901.

tion, everyday items and advertising art. He died from leukaemia at the age of 39 and is buried on the Alte →*Friedhof* in Darmstadt.

Orangery

The most gorgeous complex in the heart of →*Bessungen* is the Orangery. The terraced grounds smell deliciously, from May to October, of myrrh, lemon, fig and orange trees. Their home during the winter used to be the greenhouse of the Orangery. The hedges in the park used to screen vegetable and fruit patches, which have now disappeared, leaving more room for strolling around. Only one half of the Orangery building, drafted by Remy de la Fosse, was realised as the palace had burnt once more and finances were low. Magnificent court festivities took place in the Orangery building and the surrounding grounds. The residents of Bessungen had to remain curious bystanders until 1802, separated by the wall which fences the area off. Over time, the Orangery served many other purposes, such as a military hospital; a meeting place for the townsmen guards; a →*vivarium*; and, for thirty years, as the county →*Theatre*. In 1870, the first German show of roses opened and, in 1905,

Joseph Maria →*Olbrich* showed his blue, white, red and yellow gardens to an admiring public. The former greenhouse serves today as a well

restored ballroom where, amongst other activities, the award ceremony for the Georg-Büchner-Prize takes place every year.

The Orangery in Bessungen was built from 1719 to 1721. The small castle was originally designed to house orange trees during the winter. From May to October their scent is all over the garden.

Pädagog – Pedagogical Institute

The name already implies that learning and teaching took place here. In 1629, Georg I asked the architects, Seyfried Pfannmüller and Jakob Müller, to draft a building for the education of pupils. Higher school education began here. The Latin school offered room for four forms, a library, a music room and quarters for the teachers and the headmaster. For nearly two hundred years, pupils in Darmstadt attended the Pädagog before entering the state university in Giessen. The dilapidated school had to move to the orphanage in the neighbourhood. The Pädagog was restored by Georg →*Moller* and consequently used as a museum on local history. Today, the basement accom-

modates a restaurant and the original statue of →*Darmstadtia*. Around the corner, the Ludwig-Georgs-Gymnasium, which emerged from the Pädagog, is situated. Its building was drafted by Max Taut who tried to realise the idea of classes in the open air on a limited inner city plot. It is one out of seven Meisterbauten – Masterbuildings – which were built after an architectural competition.

Paper Theatre Collection

A special gem is hidden in a detached house on the east side of Mercksplatz: the Darmstadt Paper Theatre Collection Walter Röhler. The long title hides one of the most extensive collections of paper theatres in western Europe, encompassing about three hundred assembled stages, thousands of printed sheets and a comprehensive specialist library. For example, the complete works of the Darmstadt theatre painter, Carl Beyer, belong to the collection. The collection was donated by the Darmstadt citizen, Walter Röhler. The showcases offer an insight into the world of the theatre from the late 18th to the early 20th century. Costumes, scenery and special effects were then copied from current productions and found their way, as paper theatres, into the parlours of families. Classical productions and a large number of fairy-tales for children were staged that way. Sheets were printed with scenery, costumes and props which were then cut out and put together at home. They were sold in black and white or colour at varying prices. Depending on personal skills and tastes, the owners added light, a drawing floor, trap doors and other extras. Both adults and children played with these theatres, often with dedication, as is documented by many references. If you are lucky, you can attend one of the rare productions of a paper theatre. Everyone can, at least, take a nostalgic look at this magic world from times gone by in the museum.

Paving stones

As a matter of course we walk on paved ground through a city, not once looking down at it. But to do so

is worthwhile, as a lot can be discovered regarding the shapes, colours and patterns of the pavement itself. If you disregard the cobblestones, visible on the streets since the 16th century, and just look at the footpaths, you will notice a big variety in patterning. Most of this mosaic paving dates from the end of the 19th century, when craftsmanship was still cheap. The mosaic stones came to Darmstadt as a cheap filling of freight wagons. Large surfaces could easily be structured by using the material as ornamentation and, furthermore, pedestrians could walk on relatively dry ground. The newly-built →Martinsviertel – Martins-District, Johannesviertel, Paulusviertel and the →Mathildenhöhe are the areas where most of the mosaic pavement was laid out. If you follow the patterns, you will soon notice that entrances are emphasised or that the pattern on a building is repeated in the pavement. Some pavements give the impression of a carpet in their artistic design. Even patterns from decorative building collections were popular amongst craftsmen.

Prinze-Georg-Garden

One of the most idyllic corners in the →*Herrngarten* is the Prinze-Georg-Garden. Passing the concentrated chess players and entering the garden through a wrought-iron gate, a formal garden with a multitude of shapes is revealed. Approaching the formerly arranged plants, we see that they consist of lettuce, carrots, chard and other crops. From the end of April, people from Darmstadt come to buy the fruit and vegetables grown here, as well as a wide selection of young plants. The vegetables are not the only things that attract them to the garden; the Grand Ducal collection of bone china, which is housed in a small museum at the far end of the garden, also lures visitors. Further attractions include readings and a reading hall in the Pretlacksche' garden house, a house covered with floral paintings. The ensemble has its origins in two neighbouring garden

The portal with city arms is a relic of a villa built in 1894. It burnt down completely in 1944 and was cleared away.

plots, each with a summer house. Ludwig VIII combined the gardens and gave them as a present to his son Georg Wilhelm, who lent his name to the

place. He had it further enhanced by a tea pavilion, alcoves with stone benches and a hedge theatre. The mixed planting of flowers and crops

The 'Porcelaincastle' in the Prinz-Georgs-Garden

The outer walls of the Pretlacksche garden house are painted with trees, tendrils and garlands.

also dates from his time. Until 1829, the pleasure and kitchen gardens belonged to the Grand-Ducal family. The next hundred years were quite varied: some members of the Artists' Colony lived there and it was leased to a market garden. Today, the beauty and calm of the garden has been restored to its formal and intimate charm and is conducive to a relaxing stroll; the flower beds contain some interesting discoveries.

Rathaus – Town Hall

Opposite the market gate of the palace is the pretty Renaissance façade of the old Town Hall. Thus the sovereign and the city authorities could always keep an eye on each other. The building was draughted by Jakob Wustmann in the 16th century. Later, a stair tower was added on the

The Town Hall from the 16th century in glowing evening light

time. It was also used to house convicts who had been sentenced to death. It is not surprising that the building became too small for all these purposes and the city's administration gradually moved out during the 19th century. At first, the city parliament remained, along with the registry and local court. Today, the Town Hall is still used as a registry and on some days the area in front of it is covered in rice or petals. On the ground floor, a pub was opened at the beginning of the 20th century and it is currently run with a house brewery and the Ratskeller. Also worth a look is the 'Darmstädter Elle' – yardstick – which is located in the wall next to the entrance to the stair tower. It extends an impressive length of 24 inches and was the standard measure for all local trade until 1872.

side. The mayor; the city administration; the City Archive and the town's silver all were in the Town Hall at some

Residence

The first impression of the Residence as a well-fortified castle has to be abandoned when coming closer. The former moat still runs around the palace, but it is no longer an obstacle in entering from every direction through one of the four gates. The most magnificent gate is the wrought iron one on the market place side, achieving two floors in height. The most recently constructed entrance opens onto a modern, perspex bridge crossing the moat in the direction of the →*darmstadtium*. As diverse as the gates are the buildings inside the walls. Dainty Renaissance buildings stand next to broad Baroque façades and document a period of construction of well over 600 years. Every sovereign added or changed the Residence according to his ambitions and needs. Several big fires forced changes as well. The names of the courtyards reveal their former functions. After a successful hunt, the hunting party rode into the Course Courtyard. In the Church Courtyard, the Residence's church is situated and in the Bell Courtyard a nearly inexhaustible variety of

The Residence situated in the inner city is a complex of buildings erected over a period of 600 years. The bell tower (above) plays constantly varying melodies every quarter of an hour.

tunes rings from the Glockenspiel. The court bakery used to be in the premises of today's Castle Museum. The museum offers a good choice of costumes, furniture and carriages of Grand-Ducal times. Today, most of the Residence is used by the university and on the first weekend of July, all Darmstadt citizens celebrate their big local fair – the Heinerfest – there.

IN TE DOMINE SPERAVI

LUDOVICUS·VI·D·G·HASS

SCHLO

GRAVIVS PRINCEPS HERSFELD:

USEUM

M F

NON CONFVNDAR IN ÆTERNVM

Rosenhöhe – Roses Heights

Michael Zeyher, the master of horticulture, was summoned from Schwetzingen to Darmstadt by the Grand Duchess Wilhelmine to create an English-styled landscaped garden on the Busenberg. Wilhelmine also commissioned the first mausoleum in the garden. Her daughter, Elisabeth, had died at the age of five and she ordered the renowned architect George →*Moller* to draught a mausoleum. Subsequently, all members of the Grand-Ducal family were buried in the mausoleum. Its name Rosenhöhe – Rose Heights – became appropriate around 1900 when Grand Duke Ernst Ludwig had roses planted, as well as a rose dome and a heated water-lily

The tea-house reconstructed faithfuly to the original.

The Löwentor – Lion Gate – entrance to the Rosenhöhe.

were first on show during an exhibition on the →*Mathildenhöhe*. The path then touches a romantic tea pavilion and soon reaches, the legendary Spanish→*Tower* rises. Leaving the garden in the direction Ostbahnhof – East Station – you encounter a former archway, a relic of the time when the Grand-Ducal summer residence, Palais Rosenhöhe, still existed and relatives visiting from Russia alighted from the train at the nearby station.

pond built. The resulting change of the park was so remarkable that the term 'Darmstädter style of garden' came into use. If you walk along the paths of the Rosenhöhe, you will observe many aspects of note. To enter the garden, you have to pass under →*lions* sitting on high clinkered columns, which are nicknamed the 'sneezing hedgehogs'. They were created by Bernhard Hoetger and

The archway is the last remnant of the summer residence.

R Russian Chapel

The Russian Chapel, which is situated on the →*Mathildenhöhe* – a long way from Russian territory – is an unusual gem. Until the end of the 19th century, a classical cottage stood here. It belonged to Grand Duke Ludwig III and Grand Duchess Matilda, who lived in it during the summer. The cottage was surrounded by a landscaped garden in the English tradition.

Princess Alexandra of Hesse-Darmstadt converted to the Russian Orthodox religion to marry Tsarevitch Nicholas II. The couple frequently visited her brother, Grand Duke Ernst Ludwig, in Darmstadt. He decided to donate a plot of land to the Tsar for the construction of a private chapel. In 1897, the foundation stone was laid in the presence of numerous members of the European aristocracy including Queen Victoria and Prince Albert. A pavilion, laid out with the most precious materials, had been erected on the building site, displaying all of the building materials chosen for the chapel. From all Russian provinces, earth had been brought to Darmstadt on which to build the chapel. Louis Benois, president of the St. Petersburg Academy of Arts, was the architect. He designed the chapel in the style of traditional churches of the 16th century. The construction management was put into the hands of two local men: Gustav Jacobi and Friedrich Ollerich. Victor Wasnezow designed the mosaic pictures on the outer walls as well as the big mosaic in the apse and the murals on the interior walls. The wooden iconostasis, the precious altar cloth and the church banner are gifts from Duchess Marie of Saxe-Coburg.

The chapel, whose patron saint Mary Magdalene is mounted over the entrance portal, was consecrated in 1899 in the presence of the Tsar. Until 1938, it was still listed under his name in the land register. In 1903, the magnificent wedding of Prince Andrew of Greece to Princess Alice of →*Battenberg* took place under the eyes of the European high nobility. In 1914, the chapel was closed and all precious metal was confiscated as 'enemy property'. The service of the Russian Orthodox community takes place every fortnight.

Stadtkirche – Town Church

In and around the Town Church, the history of Darmstadt can be traced; some of it no longer easily visible. The churchyard, which used to be next to the church building, was closed after a plague epidemic in 1739. The only remaining tombstone was built into the wall of the church. It belongs to Chancellor Wolff von Todenwarth. The origins of the church go back to a Franconian funeral chapel and a St. Mary's Church. Archbishop Gerlach von Mainz gave the chapel the status of a parish church in 1369. The chapel underwent a lot of building alterations and additions, of

which those by Georg →*Moller* in the middle of the 18th century and that by the architect Karl Gruber after World War II are the most significant. Following the wishes of Landgrave Philip the Magnanimous, a Protestant service was held in the church from 1526 onwards. In the chancel an epitaph was erected commemorating the first Landgrave George I, Landgravine Magdalene zur Lippe and their ten children, in front of the oldest view of the city. To the left is a wall-mounted plaque commemorating the confirmation of the Prussian Queen, Luise, who by birth was a Darmstadt princess. In the crypts under the chancel, the tombstones of all members of the Landgravine family are situated. They can be visited only by guided tours. The oldest city arms are in the arches of the tower.

The town church was built in the late Gothic style. The epitaph Georg I dedicated to his wife Magdalena zur Lippe.

S
111

Stadtmauer – City Wall

When Darmstadt received the town charter on 23rd July 1330 from King Ludwig of Bavaria, the settlement got permission to build its own wall. It is most likely that they had a trench and an embankment or a picket trench before. Now, they began to build a city wall which was probably completed by the beginning of the 15th century. The inner part consisted of a wall one

Only smaller parts and ruins are left of the former city wall.

metre thick that reached up eight metres in height and possessed a wall-walk. This was completed by a ward and an outer wall with a trench. For further protection →*towers* were added. Some of them still survive and can be visited; the Hinkelsturm and the Weiße Turm, for instance. Time and again the wall had to be modified to make room for the steadily growing city. In the middle of the 17th century it remained intact but its protective possibilities be-

came utterly outdated and useless, as new weapons had been invented. When the new district, →*Mollerstadt*, was planned much of the city wall was demolished. Today, some remaining parts can be seen in the area of the Hinkelsturm, in Alexanderstraße and in the area of Mauerstraße. When the →*darmstadtium* was built, remains of a subterraneous listening tunnel and a tower were discovered. They were integrated into the new Congress Centre and a small exhibition on the history of the city wall was added.

St. Ludwig

George →*Moller*, who drafted the Catholic Church, St. Ludwig, noted that he would be on the safe side by maintaining the proportions of the Pantheon during his planning. It was the first Catholic church to be built in Darmstadt after the Reformation. The rotunda is impressive – if on first sight of somewhat enigmatic appearance – giving rise to a number of speculations. The shape of the rotunda, reminiscent of heathen temples and the unity of St. Ludwig, create a stately and worldly image. The main investor and client of the commonly called 'Käsglock' – cheese cover – was the Protestant Grand Duke →*Ludewig I.*

The church's cupola is 33 metres in diameter and has an overall height of 15 metres. In the eye of the dome, light is shed onto a glass sculpture, depicting the Father, the Son and the Holy Spirit. The tombstones of Grand Duchess Mathilde and Prince Friedrich of Hesse are situated in the circular colonnade that consists of 28 Corinthian columns. In the Brandnacht – night of fire – on 11th September 1944, the church burnt down to the outer walls. Reconstruction took place in 1954/55 but slight alterations had to be made due to the circumstances of the post-war period. The inside of the cupola was painted from 2003 to 2005 by Damaris Wurmdobler in 24 shades of blue, applied in seven layers. The side walls were coloured in Pompejan red. Finally a new Wintherhalter organ was purchased and now recitals in St. Ludwig are an eagerly anticipated musical event.

The impressive cupola of St. Ludwig's was built between 1822 and 1827 by Georg Moller.

Straßenbahnen und Busse – Trams and buses

Crossing Luisenplatz you cannot miss the orange-blue trams and buses frequently driving across the square. They come from all districts of Darmstadt and the surrounding area. Trams run on a track network of over 50 kilometres which is still expanding. Looking back to the origins of trams you have to go to the year 1886. Originally, two lines were in service: the →*Eberstadt* and the Griesheim line. They were puffing steam engines which were given names like 'Griesemer Lieschen' – Lizzy from Griesheim – and 'Feuriger Elias' – Fiery Elias. For the tram from Griesheim, open market carriages were constructed to transport the market women to and fro with their

A trip around the city in the historic 'Datterich-Express' is quite an experience.

The orange-blue trams cannot be overlooked in the city.

huge baskets full of vegetables and fruit from their gardens and small allotments on market days. Around ten years later, the first electric lines went into service, running from the centre to the new residential areas, and to destinations for day trips. To enlarge the range, buses were introduced in 1927. An outline of the history of trams in Darmstadt is on display in the Eisenbahnmuseum in Kranichstein – Railway Museum Kranichstein. If you want to experience what it felt like to go on a puffing steam train, look out for the regular steam days of the 'Feurige Elias' when it is running to →*Eberstadt* and Griesheim.

Technische Universität Darmstadt – Technical University of Darmstadt

On entering Darmstadt you read it on all the signs: City of Science. Surely there must have been a number of reasons, in 1997, to change the byname of Darmstadt from City of the Arts to City of Science; one of them was definitely the Technical University of Darmstadt. It took a while before Darmstadt became a university city. In 1629, the →*Pädagog* had opened its doors and it was planned to create a county university. The choice was made between Darmstadt and Gießen. Gießen was chosen, the argument being that, not only was the plot in question more quietly situated, but, also, fish from the Lahn was more easily digestible than fish from the Rhine. In 1836, the Höhere Gewerbeschule – vocational school – opened its doors. It was promoted to the rank of a technical college in 1877. From then on Abitur was required for admission. Establishing the chair for electrical engineering in 1882, and appointing Erasmus Kittler for its first professor, was an important decision for the further development of the university. Subjects like architecture, medicine, engineering, aeronautics and aviation were of major importance. Some representative buildings were erected in the town centre on the area of the former court dairy and alongside the →*Herrngarten*. Architects were Heinrich Wagner, Friedrich Pützer and Georg Wickop. In 1908, women were granted admission to university in Darmstadt. During the early years most of the women came from Eastern Europe. Growing numbers of students made new buildings necessary. As space was limited in town, the campus was divided. On the →*Lichtwiese* a second campus grew with premises for engineering, architecture and chemistry. Since 1997, the technical college can call itself Technische Universität (Technical University). About 18,000 students are enrolled there.

Theatre

The main impulse for theatre in Darmstadt developed over many centuries via the court. Most of the visitors were courtiers. Productions featured members of the princely family, their guests and, if necessary, their employees. On the occasion of weddings, baptisms or soirées they performed pastoral plays, musical comedies and charades. Every now and then, travelling theatre companies stopped over in the city and put up their stage in the marketplace. At the end of the 17th century, Landgravine Elisabeth Dorothea had a comedy house built. In the whole of Germany there were only four other separate theatre buildings at that time. For the celebration of the opening, the promi-

nent singer, Elisabeth Döbricht, was engaged. From 1800 onwards activities at the theatre became livelier. Grand Duke →Ludewig I took over the theatre company of the principal, Xavier Krebs, and built the Grand-Ducal Theatre, where 2000 visitors could be seated. Their rank decided where they were allowed to sit during performances. The programme offered mainly operas as the Grand Duke loved to conduct them himself. The theatre burnt down in the Brandnacht – night of fire – and was removed to the →Orangery in →Bessungen for nearly thirty years. Under its artistic directors, Rudolf Sellner and Gerhard Hering, the Hesse County Theatre achieved a growing fame all over Germany. From 1972 onwards, the theatre, today's Staatstheater Darmstadt, moved into its new premises at the George-Büchner-Platz. Next to it, in the former Masonic Lodge, is the stage of the Freie Szene Darmstadt e.V. The programme, offered by a variety of fringe groups, ranges from children's productions to belly dancing, magic and improvised performances.

Theatre always played an important role in the cultural life of Darmstadt.

Totenmaske – Death mask of William Shakespeare

This death mask had a long and adventurous journey before it reached Darmstadt. It first entered Germany in the 18th

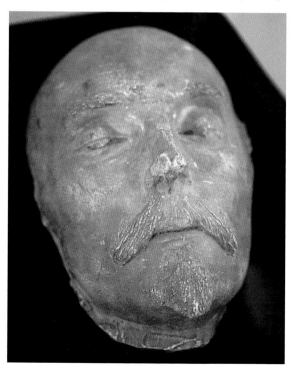

century with the Mayence capitular, Franz Graf Kesselstatt. After his death, his belongings were auctioned and the Darmstadt painter, Ludwig Becker, purchased the mask; that was its first visit to Darmstadt. Ludwig Becker took it on a journey to England and lent it to the British Museum while he travelled in Australia. Following Becker's death, the mask was returned to his relatives in Darmstadt. In 1960, it was put up for auction again and the →*University* and State Library purchased it, since which time it has been kept in the collection of the library. The mask is thought to be authentic because there is an impression of a growth next to the left eye which is the result of a rare disease from which Shakespeare is known to have suffered. Two pictures of him which are proved genuine show the same phenomenon. This was researched by doctors and experts of the Federal Criminal Police Office.

Towers

Whether you look up to or down from a tower it always offers a worthwhile change of perspective. Darmstadt has quite a range of different

The 'Weiße Turm' (left) was built as a defence tower and part of the city wall in the 15th century. The 'Hinkelsturm' (above) belongs to the remains of the the former city wall.

towers inviting a visit or an ascent. To start with there is the Weiße Turm – White Tower – in the centre of town. The name goes back some 300 years and is probably due to the white plaster on the outside walls. Decorated with a crested roof, it has a defiant character. It has served as part of the fortification, as a gaol and even as The Treasury; in fact it has fulfilled more or less every use a tower can have. Today, the Darmstädter Film and Photo Club has its premises behind the walls which are 1.7m thick. Only a short distance away the Hinkelsturm – 'Hen Tower' – is situated. Its name derives from a huge menhir which still lays in the Hinkelsgasse. Originally, it formed part of the city wall and was inhabited until a hundred years ago. Like all the other towers it was part of the fire watch kept by the citizens. Today the Old Town Museum is in its remnants. On several floors a model of the old town and historical displays can be studied. From the top floor the view over the roofs of the city is impressive. Taking a walk across →Rosenhöhe in an easterly direction, you will encounter a rather mysterious tower: the Spanish Tower. It is uncertain who had it built and for what purpose. Rumour has it that it was built to be able to watch military exercises or that courtiers met here for an idyllic cup of tea. But then, who invented the name?

The 'Spanische Turm' on the Rosenhöhe

ULB – University and State Library

Many rooms of the →*Residence* are in use today as reading rooms, store rooms and other library facilities. They are open every day between 8am and 2pm for anyone interested. The library was opened to the public in 1817 when Ludwig X decreed it. The first books came from a princely collection. Else of Katzenelnbogen determined in the 14th century in her marriage contract that she was to inherit her husband's library after his death. This included, amongst other books, a Titurel by Wolfram von Eschenbach. When the first acquisitions were made under Georg I in 1568, the history of the library began. During the following centuries it remained a court library where the sovereigns' interests and dedication copies influenced its contents. The only readers were courtiers. In 1803, the stock increased rapidly as secularised abbey libraries were incorporated into the collection. The library was opened to the general public from 1817. In 1902, Darmstadt's library was among the nine biggest in the German Reich. War damage halved its stock as well as the stock of the library of the Technische Hochschule; hence, they were combined as Landes- und Hochschulbibliothek – State and College Library. Since 1994, the library has been connected to the →*Technische Universität Darmstadt* and is now called University and State Library and it keeps around 1.6m books and 6,800 periodicals in stock. The collection encompasses incunables like the Hitda Codex and the Gero Codex; a musical library with 4,774 autographs; a collection on the history of →*theatre* in Darmstadt and any kind of book required for research and study at the Technische Universität Darmstadt.

Under the city: Tunnels and drains

There is no large river flowing through Darmstadt and everything seems to be built solidly on stone. But appearances are deceptive: under the hill of →*Mathildenhöhe,* as well as under most of the inner city, there expands a system of tunnels and drains. This used to include caverns and tunnels built as escape routes running from the palace under the old city wall and to town church. Due to building activities over the centuries, most of them are no longer accessible. However, one, the old brewers' canal, can be visited on a guided tour. The origins of the canal probably date back to the construction of a water pipe in the 17th century, commissioned by the landgrave. From the east of Darmstadt, where water was plentiful, fresh water was directed to municipal wells. In the middle of the 19th century, two things happened: space in the →*breweries* situated in the old part of town grew sparse and a new brewing method was invented that demanded changes in production sites, bottom-fermented beer. There were already 29 registered breweries

in business at the time. But the demand grew steadily and, as opportunities to build ice and fermenting cellars into the hill of Mathildenhöhe arose, more breweries opened. Twelve breweries found locations under the Mathildenhöhe. Ice was chopped in the →*Woog* during winter and then filled through the holes into the caverns. Temperatures remained between 8-10 degrees Celsius underground, which was cold enough for the fermentation process. The melting water went out through the old water pipes. A ventilation system completed the installations. Special attractions are the 584 metres of tunnels and an ice cellar shaped like a dome.

Vivarium

Reactions in Darmstadt were rather sceptical when the suggestion was made, in 1928, to establish a Zoo. Professor List commented that a Zoo in Darmstadt was impossible and would never survive. He emphasised his statement by quoting that not even the Zoo in a capital like Munich had been able to survive because of lack of interest from the general public. Nevertheless, the first Zoo was opened in 1956 in Darmstadt under the management of Dr. Heinz Ackermann. It began in the ramshackle greenhouses of the city nursery in the →Orangery in →Bessungen. Originally, about thirty aquariums and terrariums existed which were mainly visited by school classes. When the 'school pavilion' was closed due to disrepair, the magistrate of Darmstadt decided on a new site in 1962. The Vivarium moved to its current place opposite the →Botanical Gardens, an area covering well over four hectares. From 1965, visitors could once again look at the terrariums and

On four hectares situated to the east of the city over 700 animals can be seen like the binturongs (above left), flamingos and their offspring and the enormous yak.

aquariums. In the following years many new enclosures were added. Animals, ranging from wading birds and bearcats to black macaque moved into the Vivarium. Walking through the Vivarium today, you en- counter 700 animals from 150 species. There is a small zoo school as well. The Vivarium successfully takes part in national and international breeding programs for endangered species.

Waldspirale – Forest Helix

Looking over the roofs of Darmstadt, the eye suddenly gets caught by two golden cupolas, and memories of the stories of The Arabian Nights are

evoked. Even on a second viewing, they do not turn out to be fata morganas. Two golden cupolas top the forest helix, one of the fairy-tale buildings of the Viennese artist Friedensreich Hundertwasser. Approaching the building, you can discern a wooded helix on a multi-layer foundation that is reminiscent of the layers of earth on which the house is built. Ceramic pillars in a multitude of shapes support and decorate the house; a small creek bubbles across curved paths; windows seem to be spread like dancers over the façade. Some window borders have been coloured as far as a brush could reach by the tenants – a right granted in their contract. The building was completed in 2000 after the death of Friedensreich Hundertwasser and is one out of 25 ob-

The 'Waldspirale' – forest helix – is an unusual residential house with 105 flats designed by Friedensreich Hundertwasser.

jects he drafted. The basic concept is to return as much to the earth as has been

taken from it by every building. Thus, a great number of plants found a home on the roof and in recesses of the façade. Hundertwasser commented on the forest helix as being a house supportive to nature and the dreams of mankind re presenting the increase of nature in the city. From the café on the roof the view reaches all over Darmstadt and as far as Frankfurt on clear days.

Wella Museum

Beauty and its manifold nuances is a topic mankind has been interested in for a long time. Therefore, it is only consequent that a company like Wella, the manufacturer of beauty products, has acquired an extensive collection on all fields of beauty and personal hygiene. As Wella's headquarters are situated in Darmstadt, it seemed only logical, in 1952, to open their museum here. In 2003, a completely new design for their exposition was created to offer an attractive setting for more than 300 exhibits. The display includes items of high cultural and historical interest, ranging from combs from ancient Greece to a

statuette of the Egyptian God Nefertem. The presentation in the showcases covers six subject areas: Skin Care and Personal Hygiene; Decorative Cosmetics; Fragrance and Perfume; The Hairdressing Profession; Beards and Shaving and Hair. It goes without saying that a comprehensive display of 125 years of the company's history is there as well. Elaborate lighting turns a visit' to the museum into an experience for the eye.

Wolfskehlscher Garten

Today the eye only encounters a gentle slope in the Wolfskehlscher Garten. In former times it used to be a vineyard location with a great reputation. The hill is also known among the population as the Gallows Hill dating from the time when the gallows of the tithe district used to be situated on the unsettled ground between Bessungen and Darmstadt. By the end of the 18th century it was taken down when hangings ceased. The apothecary Girsch, planted an orchard and commissioned a Biedermeier tea-house. One hundred years later the respected Jewish banker, Otto von Wolfskehl, had a Wilhelminian villa built for his family to live in. The teahouse survived until today and has passers-by on their way through the quiet park indulge in romantic fantasies. A copy of the statue of the patron of the city, →*Darmstadtia*, by Karl Buchert was erected in 1964. The original is on display in the basement of the →*Pädagog*. If there is sufficient snow during the winter, the slope resounds with the voices of children and teenagers using it for a fast ride on their toboggan.

Woog

Only the Große Woog – large pond – is still easy to find nowadays. The Kleine Woog – small pond – was dried up and is used as a parking lot now. The word 'Woog' describes water of any kind and has been in use in Darmstadt since 1568, the beginning of the reign of Georg I. Both Woogs were dug to stop the frequent flooding by the Darmbach, which caused serious damage to the houses and bridges in the old town, as well as to build a water reservoir for fighting fires and to serve as a pond for fish farming. Nutrition in

East of the old city stretches the 'Große Woog' which has been used for swimming since 1820.

those days included many days of fasting a year: hence a lot of fish was eaten. During the 16th century, a 'Woogsfleet' is documented as fishing in the pond. Many festivities, ranging from ice-skating during the winter to fantastic sea battles performed to amuse the courtiers, took place on the

Woog. Swimming only came into fashion at the end of the 18th century. At first, the military dipped into the water, which caused annoyance, for the state did not have enough money to supply every soldier with swimming trunks! From 1828 onwards, a bathhouse, a swimming pier and a pleasure island were built, which were used until 1927 by men and women separately.

The lifeguard on duty received 1 guilder for the recovery of a drowned person. If he recovered them alive he did not get any money. The Große Woog has belonged to the city since 1935 and has been enlarged for swimming galas. Going for a swim in the heart of Darmstadt is one of the special pleasures of the city, one which Goethe indulged in with some friends.

Zentralbad –
Central swimming pool

Swimming and bathing are nowadays usually connected with well-being and sport. At the time of the construction of today's Jugendstilbad, attitudes were different. Around 1900, most households in Darmstadt did not have their own bathrooms. The magistrate ordered that a public indoor swimming pool, including bathrooms, should be built, to offer citizens the opportunity to take a thorough scrub at least once a week. August Buxbaum was commissioned to plan it. The result was a public swimming bath with separate pools for men and women – segregation of the sexes was still taken for granted –, 37 baths, a laundry and a dog parlour. Both World Wars led to changes: during World War I, the swimming pool

The 'Zentralbad' was renovated extensively during the last few years.

for men was covered with planks and uniforms were sewn on top of it. In World War II, the women's swimming pool burnt down. Over the past few years, the Zentralbad has been restored and turned into a gem. The historic architecture of the front was renovated and the tower received a copper hood again. Inside, a colourful population of octopuses, fish and fabulous water creatures is romping about on walls and ceilings. The swimming hall is shining with Jugendstil ornaments, surrounded by stuccoed promenades. A special oasis was created with treats like a brine pool and a Turkish Bath. On mellow summer

The Zentralbad was built from 1907 to 1909. It displays numerous decorative elements in the Jugendstil.

evenings you can enjoy the view over Darmstadt from the roof terrace with an outside pool.

Sources

Karl Ackermann: Von der Wasser-
burg zur Großstadt, Darmstadt 1964

Corinna Bartsch, Thomas Becker: Vivarium, Darmstadts Tiergarten,
Darmstadt 1998

Bessunger Interessengemeinschaft
(Hg.): 1000 Jahre Bessungen, Darmstadt 2002

Heiner Boehncke, Peter Brunner,
Hans Sarkowicz: Die Büchners,
Frankfurt 2008

Hermann Bürnheim, Jürgen Burmeis-
ter: Bahnen und Busse rund um den
Langen Ludwig, Düsseldorf 1997

Bettina Clausmeyer-Ewers: Prinz-
Georgs-Garten, Regensburg 2004

Denkmalschutz in Darmstadt: Eva
Reinhold-Postina: Das Darmstädter
Hallenbad, Darmstadt 1995

Michael Groblewski: St. Ludwig in
Darmstadt, Regensburg 2005

Horst-Volker Henschel: Darmstadts
„Unterwelt", Darmstadt 2007

Historischer Verein für Hessen (Hg):
Stadtlexikon Darmstadt, Darmstadt
2006

Friedel Kirschner: Eberstadts
Geschichte – kurzgefasst – von 782
bis 1998, Darmstadt 1998

Kulturamt der Stadt Darmstadt (Hg):
Kunst im öffentlichen Raum in Darmstadt 1641–1994, Darmstadt 1995

Landesamt für Denkmalpflege Hessen (Hg): Denkmaltopografie der
Stadt Darmstadt, Wiesbaden 1994

Irmgard Lehn: Historisches Pflaster,
Darmstadt 1993

Eberhard Lohmann: Landgraf Georg I.
und die Anfänge von Kranichstein,
Darmstadt 2003

Sibylle Maxheimer, Sabine Welsch:
Geheimnisvolles Darmstadt, Gu-
densberg-Gleichen 2002

Adolf Müller: Der Große Woog zu
Darmstadt, Darmstadt 1934

Barbara Obermüller, Karin Diegel-
mann: Orte der Ruhe und der Kraft,
Darmstadt 2003

Eva Reinhold-Postina/Nikolaus Heiss:
Darmstädter Architekturgeschichte
in 5 Bänden, Darmstadt 1994

Stefan Schneckenburger. Botanis-
cher Garten der Technischen Universität Darmstadt, Darmstadt 1999

Carlo Schneider: Die Friedhöfe in
Darmstadt, Darmstadt 1991

Dr. Georg Seide: Die Russisch Ortho-
doxe Kirche der Hl. Maria Magdalena auf der Mathildenhöhe in
Darmstadt, Ottobrunn 1997

Technische Universität Darmstadt:
Technische Bildung in Darmstadt.
Die Entwicklung der Technischen
Hochschule 1836–1996 (6 Bde.),
Darmstadt 2000

Wissenschaftsstadt Darmstadt (Hg):
Die Russische Kapelle, Darmstadt
2007
Hanne Wittmann: Die Löwen von
Darmstadt, Darmstadt 1990

Contents

Achteckiges Haus 10
Arheilgen 12
Battenberg 14
Peter Behrens 15
Bessungen 16
Botanical Gardens 19
Breweries..................... 20
Büchner 21
Central Station for Electric Light 22
Matthias Claudius 24
Darmstadtia 25
darmstadtium 26
Datterich 28
Eberstadt 30
Electric and other trains 32
Empfindsamkeit 34
The Felsings – a dynasty 36
Fraa Liebig 38
Frankenstein 40
Friedhöfe – Cemeteries 42
Gas and water 44
Gefängnis – Gaol 46
Haus der Geschichte – House of History 47
Haus für Industriekultur –
House for Industrial Culture 50
Herrngarten 52
Hessisches Landesmuseum –
Hessian State Museum 54
Jagdschloss Kranichstein –
The hunting lodge Kranichstein 56
Justiz – Justice 60
Kollegiengebäude – Council Hall 63
Lichtwiese – Meadow of Light 64
Literaturhaus – House of Literature .. 65
Löwen – Lions 66
Ludewig and Luise 68
Marketplace 72
Martinsviertel 74
Mathildenhöhe 76
Merck 82
Moller City 84
Neufert's residence for singles 86
Olbrich 87
Orangery 90
Pädagog – Pedagogical Institute 92
Paper Theatre Collection 93
Paving Stones 94
Prinz-Georg-Garden 95
Rathaus – Town Hall 98
Residence 100
Rosenhöhe – Roses Heights 104
Russian Chapel 106
Stadtkirche – Town Church 110
Stadtmauer – City Wall 112
St. Ludwig 114
Straßenbahnen und Busse –
Trams and buses 116
Technische Universität Darmstadt -
Technical University of Darmstadt ... 118
Theatre 120
Totenmaske –
Death Mask of William Shakespeare . 121
Towers 122
ULB – University and State Library ... 124
Under the city: Tunnels and drains ... 125
Vivarium 126
Waldspirale – Forest Helix 128
Wella Museum 130
Wolfskehlscher Garden 132
Woog 134
Zentralbad – Central swimming pool .. 136

Cover photographs: Langer Ludwig, House of History, Orangery and Rosenhöhe
Endpaper front: Entrance to Rosenhöhe, the gatekeeper's lodge
Endpaper back: Town plan

Photos: page 44 © Nikolaus Heiss; page 130,131 © Wella-Museum

Bibliographic information published by the Deutsche Nationalbibliothek
The Deutsche Nationalbibliothek lists this publication in the Deutsche Nationalbibliografie;
detailed bibliografic data are available in the Internet at http://dnb.d-nb.de

Translation by Anja Spangenberg assisted by Keverne Weston und Pete Old

© 2010 by Husum Druck- und Verlagsgesellschaft mbH u. Co. KG,
   Husum
Gesamtherstellung: Husum Druck- und Verlagsgesellschaft
Postfach 1480, D-25804 Husum – www.verlagsgruppe.de
ISBN 978-3-89876-493-3

1 Achteckiges Haus
2 Central Station for Electric Light
3 darmstadtium
4 Datterich fountain
5 Goethe statue
6 Gaol
7 Statue of Georg I.
8 House of History
9 Hessian State Museum
10 Herrngarten
11 Law Court
12 Council Hall
13 House of Literature
14 Fraa Liebig
15 Langer Ludwig
16 Mathildenhöhe
17 Peter Behrens
18 Moller City
19 Marketplace
20 Martinsviertel/Alte Vorstadt
21 Neufert's residence for singles
22 Orangery
23 Olbrich-House
24 Pädagog/Pedagogial Institute
25 Paper Theatre Collection
26 Porzellanmuseum
27 Residence
28 Town Hall
29 Rosenhöhe/Roses Heights
30 St. Ludwig
31 Town Church
32 City Wall
33 Technical University of Darmstadt
34 White Tower
35 Theatre
36 Russian Chapel
37 Universitäts- und
   Landesbibliothek/University and
   State Library
38 Woog
39 Zentralbad/
   Central swimming pool
40 former house of he parents of
   Georg Büchner

142